Fulfillment By Amazon For Beginners

Step-by-step Instructions On How To Make An Income With Amazon FBA

By Argena Olivis

www.ArgenaOlivis.com

[Bonus] Download Your Amazon FBA Bundle Creation Course + Video On How To Get Approved In Gated Categories

In the Amazon bundles mini-course, you'll learn how to create bundles for Amazon FBA, which leads to a more stable business model and less competition.

Also, get our free video on how to get approved in categories. You'll need this to take your business to the next level.

To Get Access Visit:
http://www.argenaolivis.com/fbaebook

Table Of Contents

Introduction

I want to thank you and congratulate you for downloading the book, *"Fulfillment By Amazon For Beginners: Step By Step Instructions On How To Make An Income With Amazon FBA"*.

This book contains proven steps and strategies on how to start your Amazon FBA business from scratch.

Amazon is the biggest e-commerce site ever. People go there to shop. They have their credit cards ready and on file with Amazon because they trust them.

When people visit Amazon they're looking to buy. It's like Google for buyers.

This is why now is a great time to start using Amazon's platform to start your own Amazon FBA business.

It's a pretty simple process once you know what to do, but when you're first starting out things can be complicated.

You need to know that you're signing up correctly and you need to make sure you have the right materials to send your first shipment into Amazon.

I remember when I was sending my first shipment into Amazon; I was freaking out trying to piece together information. I was searching for YouTube videos to walk me through exactly what to do but found that there was none.

That's exactly why I put together this guide to walk you through the process when you're first beginning. The great thing about this is that each chapter is step by step and forces you to take action.

It's obvious Amazon has a great platform, and if you know what you're doing you can use Amazon as a vehicle to supplement or replace the income at a job.

Where you want to take your Amazon business is up to you. I use my Amazon income as a way to diversify my income as an online business owner.

Amazon is a great vehicle that I know works; you'll be surprised at how fast you can make money if you follow the right system.

Fulfillment by Amazon for beginners is a complete guide that will walk you through step by step how to get started.

It's great that you've decided to invest in this guide before beginning so you'll know what to do and what to expect when you start selling.

I hope you're ready to take some action. The way to get the most out of this book is to take action on the steps as you read them.

Thanks again for downloading this book, I hope you enjoy it!

information is without contract or any type of guarantee assurance.

The trademarks that are used are without any consent, and the publication of the trademark is without permission or backing by the trademark owner. All trademarks and brands within this book are for clarifying purposes only and are the owned by the owners themselves, not affiliated with this document.

This book is in no way affiliated with Amazon.com and is just my personal account of selling on Amazon.

Chapter 1: Setting Up Your Amazon Account

Welcome and congratulations on taking a leap to start selling on Amazon. The first thing you need to do is set up your Amazon seller account.

This process will take about 15 minutes.

Before you get started, you'll need a few things.

What you'll need:

- email address,
- credit card or bank card
- physical US address
- phone number
- EIN or Social Security Number
- bank account
- routing number of bank

Visit <u>www.sellercentral.amazon.com</u> to sign up. You'll come across a blue box that says "Not already selling on Amazon", click on the blue link that says "Register Now".

Then you'll come to a page that prompts you to choose rather you want to sell as a professional or an individual.

Sometimes Amazon may run promotions where you get one

month free when you sign up for a professional account.

A professional account at this time is about $40 a month and may be worth investing in because there are many benefits.

Benefits Of Having A Professional Amazon Account:

- won't be charged the $0.99 per sale of an item (if you plan on selling more than 40 items a month get a pro account)

- ability to download data such as spreadsheets, inventory lists, and reports

- tools for managing and listing multiple items

- ability to get the "buy box" button

- able to ungate categories that you're restricted in

- ability to create promo codes and discounts for your items

If you are just dabbling in FBA, choose the individual account and you won't be charged the $40 monthly fee.

Keep in mind that you can change your plan at any time, nothing is set in stone.

Once you choose the plan you want to go with, you'll be asked to log in.

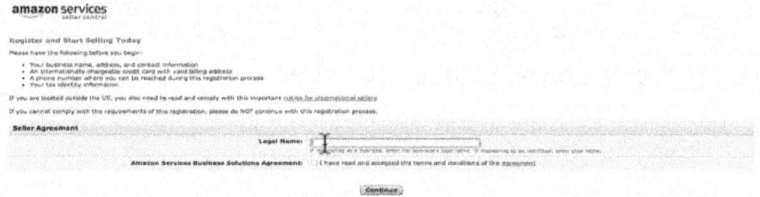

If you already have an Amazon account as a buyer, you can simply use that same email address.

After logging in, you'll come to a screen that asks for your legal name. Type your name or the name of your business in the box. If you already have an LLC or Corporation that you want to sell under enter the name of your company.

Read the terms of agreement and then check the box beside it that says "I have accepted the terms and conditions of the agreement". Then click continue.

Next you'll come to the registration page. Fill in all the areas.

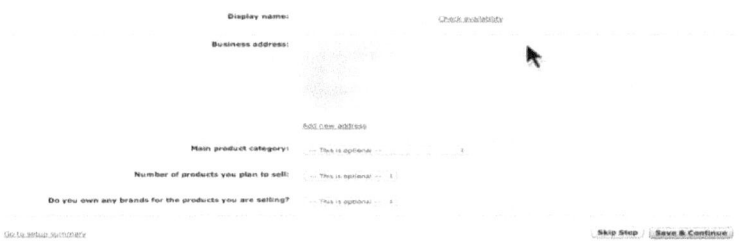

<u>Display name</u>- This is the name customers will see when they choose to buy from you. You can come back and change this at any time. You're able to check the availability of the display name you choose by clicking the link beside the box that says "check availability".

<u>Business Address</u>- You can use your home address unless you have a warehouse or brick and mortar business.

They also have some optional sections you can fill out such as:

- your main product category

- number of products you plan on selling

- if you own the brands of the products you'll be selling

When it comes to the main product category option, if you are planning to sell in only a particular niche you may want to choose what category you'll be focusing on.

But when you're just getting started you may want to leave these options blank because you can always go back to your account settings and change them at a later date.

Once you choose your display name and business address, click the button that says "save and continue".

Next you'll come to the screen where they want your credit card information. Fill out this section and hit "save and continue".

Then you'll come to the screen where Amazon asks to verify your identity. You can have them call you or send you a text message with the pin number you'll be prompted to enter.

After you're finished the screen will say "phone verification complete". Click the "continue" button.

Next, enter all the necessary tax information they ask for and click the "complete registration" button.

Then you're all set. You now have your Amazon seller account set up. Way to go! If you ever want to log back into your account, make sure to visit www.sellercentral.amazon.com and log in.

Now we can move on to what materials you're going to need to start selling. Please do not move on to the next chapter without taking action first.

Chapter 2: Materials You'll Need To Start Selling

Amazon FBA is a business that deals with physical products, printing, shipping, labeling, and there will be some start-up costs when starting out.

I like to think of it as the cost of doing business. There will always be fees and there's no such thing as making money without spending money. There are always fees involved no matter what type of business you want to pursue.

The startup cost for Amazon FBA is cheap compared to getting started with some other types of businesses. And keep in mind that Amazon is allowing you to get in front of millions of customers that you wouldn't have the resources to reach otherwise.

Do not let things such as start-up costs hold you back from making money and having your own business. Amazon has millions of customers, and you'll be using their traffic and customer service to sell your stuff, so some fees ought to be involved.

If you are going through hard times and don't have the money, you may be able to improvise, but it'll be an easier journey if you start off with the right things so you can get your business off the ground fast.

I've created a printable checklist that tells you exactly what you'll need to start off with. You can download it by visiting: http://www.argenaolivis.com/wp-content/uploads/2014/10/fbachecklist.pdf

Laser Jet Printer or Thermal Label Printer

You're going to need either a laser jet printer or a thermal printer because Amazon does not allow you to use inkjet printers for your labels. They do not allow ink jet printers because the label can get smudged and become unreadable when items get to the warehouse.

A way to get around this is to put clear tape over the label if you're using an ink jet printer. I personally use the DYMO LabelWriter 450 and it works great.

DYMO LabelWriter 450

When setting up your DYMO printer make sure to use the registration CD that comes along with the printer. Also, download adobe reader (free) to your computer.

Before I was using ListLabelShip (described below) I would open the list of labels in Adobe Reader and capture the image of the label using the actual Dymo App on my computer by using the "screen grab" option.

You may want to look into tools such as www.listlabelship.com in order to make life easier. It's only $5.00 a month at this moment in time. This tool allows you to print labels for items as you list them. This is a good thing because it's time-consuming to print out sheets of labels and find which label goes on which product.

Labels

You'll also need labels to put on your items so when they get to the fulfillment center they're able to scan them in. FBA requires your labels to be removable.

If you're using a laser printer you'll need the Avery 30 label sheets. If you're using the DYMO LabelWriter 450, use the DYMO labels. Keep in mind that if you decide to go with the

DYMO that you'll only have to purchase labels and not ink.

If you don't want to buy a printer or labels, you also have the option for Amazon to label them for you. It'll cost $0.20 an item.

Don't throw out your ink jet printer just yet, you'll still need it and some white paper to print out the packing slips for the outside of the box. You can get free box labels at UPS for free with a free account.

Tape

You're going to need a tape gun to tape your boxes at the bottom and top so items won't fall out. You'll also need regular clear tape to tape items and help seal stretch wrap.

Scissors

Any scissors will do. You need these to cut tape at times, cut the box labels, cut stretch wrap, and anything else the comes up during packaging.

Scale

You need a scale to weigh the boxes before you send them into Amazon so they can tell you how much shipping is going to cost. The best type of scale is the ones that have the reader attached to the outside so you can see how much a box weights without having to move the box to see the numbers.

Make sure the scale you get can weigh a box up to fifty pounds because fifty pounds is the heaviest size a box can be when sent to the fulfillment center.

Boxes

You need boxes in order to package your product to send them to Amazon. You may be able to get free boxes at your local store, just keep a lookout. But you can always purchase boxes from stores like Wal-Mart and Home Depot.

Amazon Seller App

You're going to need a smartphone to source products in the store. Use the Amazon Seller App to find the rank, price, and number of sellers for a particular product.

To get the app, go to your app store and download it onto your smartphone, it's completely free. You also get to see how many products you've sold and it has a database where you can view the past products you've scanned and view your inventory.

Scotty Peelers

You'll need Scotty Peelers to remove stickers from the products you're going to sell. This will save you time, the silver one works the best.

Goo Gone

You're going to want to use Goo Gone along with the Scotty Peelers. After you remove a sticker there's going to be sticky residue left over, Goo Gone removes it easily if you spray some on the item and wipe it clean with a rag.

Be cautious when spraying a lot of Goo Gone on cardboard boxes. You don't want to destroy the packaging.

Suffocation Stickers

Amazon lets you know that you need Suffocation Stickers on bags that have a 3" or more sized opening. This is so that you can protect yourself if a child chokes or suffocates for the bag you put their product in.

You also have the option to print these if you don't want to buy the stickers. Or you can buy bags with the suffocation warning already on them.

Poly Bags

Poly bags are needed to put items such as CD's, DVD's, Toys, and more. Your items need to be protected while in the fulfillment center. And the customer gets a better buying experience when items are packaged correctly. Make sure to buy the clear kind so your labels can be scanned.

Stretch Wrap

You're going to need stretch wrap to protect items when having them shipped out.

Box Re-sizer

You're going to need a box re-sizer to fit as many items as you can in one box to save on shipping costs.

Filler

Sometimes your box can't be filled all the way to the top so you'll need material such as newspaper and bubble wrap to keep the items secure in the box so they don't move around and get damaged during transit. So make sure to keep all your old newspaper.

Scanner

A scanner is optional and you can always get it later on in your business. A scanner is used to look up products with speed. But when searching for a product on Amazon you can always type in the number under the barcode.

As you can see, there's going to be an upfront investment to start this business. But the sooner you get started, the faster you'll be able to make your money back. All you have to do is take action!

Make sure to keep your receipts for all these items you purchased above so you can write them off in your taxes. Also, make sure to keep receipts of any inventory you purchase.

Now that you have all the times you need we're going to find some products to list on Amazon. When you're just starting out you want to start sourcing products around your house, this way you can get a feel for how to send in a shipment.

The next best thing for a new Amazon FBA business owner is to do either retail arbitrage or sourcing at thrift stores.

Chapter 3: Sourcing For Products To List

Sourcing is also known as scouting, reselling, retail arbitrage, picking, and more. There are so many names for it, but it doesn't matter what you call it, business is business.

The first thing you want to do is download the Amazon Seller App and start scanning stuff around your house to sell. To download this app you'll need a smartphone.

When I first started my box was full of items I had around my house that had a bar code and I wasn't using. You'll be surprised how much new stuff you have laying around and how much it's worth.

And since I started my Amazon FBA journey, every time I go into a store I go to the clearance section to see if there was anything worth getting.

The idea here is to buy low and sell high. The first thing you do is scan the object to see if it's listed on Amazon, if it's not then you may want to create a listing for it later, but when you're first starting out find items that are already listed to speed up the process of getting your first shipment out to Amazon.

You want to sell an item for at least 3 times as much as the price you pay for it. Once you scan the item the Amazon Seller app will tell you what the rank of the item is, the highest price the item is going for on FBA, and how many FBA sellers there are (both FBA and merchant fulfilled).

If there are no FBA sellers, you're in luck. You can see how many merchant fulfilled people are selling it for and double or even triple the price. You can do this because Amazon has prime members that are willing to pay more to get their item within two days.

You want to pay close attention to the rank. Try to list things with a rank of 100,000 or less. The lower the rank on an item the more it's selling.

You can find products to sell at:

- big box stores

- thrift stores

- yard sales

- online

There are always going to be places to find low priced products. You just have to keep a lookout.

Thrift stores are a great place to start. Keep in mind that thrift stores like the Goodwill restock new items every day because there are always new people donating things. So every day you'll have a chance to find something great.

Media items such as CD's and DVD's are always best if you can find them new and still in its package. This will decrease the amount of returns. When it comes to DVD's you now have to get approved to sell them because Amazon has them in a gated category (scroll down to the bottom of this book to get my video on how to get approved in categories on Amazon).

This means if you find DVD's around your house that you want to sell you may first have to find some low priced ones at a retail store and get three receipts for them so you can get approved to sell in that category.

You also have the opportunity to do online arbitrage. You can find low-priced products online to sell, get them sent to you, and then list them for a higher price on Amazon.

There are tons of great find out there, you just have to know where to look. The best time to start looking is now.

But let's start with the items in your house. Get these listed first so you can get comfortable with the process of sending your products to the fulfillment centers.

Chapter 4: Listing Products

Okay, now I'm assuming you've gathered some items around your house and you're ready to list them on Amazon.

Log into your seller account by visiting www.sellercentral.amazon.com

On the top navigation bar, you'll see "inventory". Hover over the word "inventory" and it will become a drop down menu. Select "add a product".

The following directions are for when using your personal computer, not your smartphone:

Grab one of your products and look for the bar code. Type the 12 digit barcode into the box that says "find it on Amazon" and click the search button. If you have a scanner, simply scan the barcode and then click the search button.

If the item is already listed on Amazon, you'll see a product or similar products pop up. Select "see all product details" link underneath the one that looks just like your product.

The product page will open in a new screen. The next thing we want to do is look directly underneath the description and click the small blue link that has a number and says new or used next to it. For example: 89 new from $9.99 and 25 used from $6.99.

165 new   14 used from $66.00

If you have a new product to list, select the link that says new. If used, select used. Next we want to see how we're going to price our items according to other FBA sellers. Typically you want to match the same low price as other FBA sellers so you can possibly get the buy box (keep in mind that you have to be a pro seller to be eligible for the buy box).

But if you know your item is worth more, and you're a little more patient, you can price it a little higher. Do not price your items lower than the lowest FBA price. All this does is creates a price war and no one wins!

To decipher the lowest and highest prices for FBA items, click on the checkbox that says "show prime offers only" or "free shipping" at the top. Then you'll be able to see other sellers (if there are any FBA sellers). FBA sellers will have their delivery status as "fulfillment by Amazon" beside the seller name.

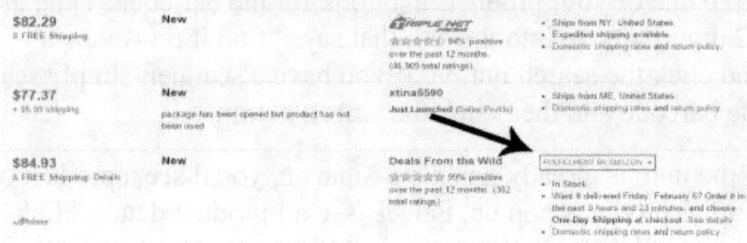

The prices will go from lowest to highest.

Now go back to your Amazon seller account tab. If the item is correct, click on the button beside it that says "sell yours".

You'll then come to a screen that has a form. You only need to fill out the information with the red star beside it.

Select your item's condition in the drop down menu.

Condition Notes

Be very thorough with your condition notes so you can stand out from other sellers. If your items are used, go the extra step and upload a picture of it so the customer can be certain what they are receiving.

You want to add condition notes to your listings to make them more appealing to potential customers. Some won't even look at the condition notes because they think their item will be coming straight from Amazon (especially if they're buying it new), they'll just click the buy box.

But others look at things such as condition notes, feedback percentages, and more.

It all depends, but you want to make sure your item gets picked over the competitors. Here are some examples of things you may want to add to your condition notes:

- packaged carefully

- free 2-day shipping

- expiration date _____

- tested (for used games/CDs/DVDs)

- bubble wrapped

- poly bagged

- fresh batteries included (you'd have to go out and buy some new batteries)

Now back to the Amazon listing process: Next, type in the price you'll be selling the item for. Go to the very bottom of the form where it says Shipping option and select "I want Amazon to provide customer service for my items if they sell".

Then click the button at the very bottom that says "save and finish".

Then you'll be prompted to create a new shipping plan. Packing type "individual products".

On the next screen, you'll see your product listed. Type in the quantity of the product you have.

The go back to the inventory tab and add the rest of your products. Make sure to add the other products to the existing shipping plan by using the drop down menu when you go through the process again.

Keep in mind that you want to add as many products as possible in order to save on shipping, the more you ship at one time the better.

Also, to avoid your products going to too many different fulfillment centers, make sure you list all your products in one sitting if you can.

Okay, now that you have all your products listed for that shipment click the continue button.

Amazon will ask you for the address that you'll be shipping the items from, add your address.

Next, they'll let you know if any of the products you've listed have special "prep" requirements. This has to do with the way Amazon wants you to pack the items. If so, take note and click the continue button.

Some of the suggestion Amazon may ask for prep are:

- bag an item

- box an item

- bubble wrap an item

- etc.

Then you want to print out the labels for your products. We'll go more into that in the next chapter.

Chapter 5: Packing and Setting Up Shipment

You have to clean and prep products before labeling them, or do it as you list them each individually, whatever works best for you.

Make sure you take off all price tags; this is where the Scotty Peeler comes in handy. Clean off the sticky residue from the price tags using Goo Gone or a similar product.

Take your time when peeling stickers off the item, because you don't want to damage the item. You also don't want the item to look dingy or used where the price tag used to be.

Once again, be careful when using Goo Gone on cardboard boxes. It can melt away some of the box itself making the product look used.

Look for the barcode on each item and put the label you've printed over the existing barcode (directly on the item). If the item is new, do not open it, simply place your label over the barcode.

The barcode should be scannable. Do not put it on any edges of products. If the product is too small for the label, bag it and put the label on the outside of a clear poly bag.

If the label is too big for where the product's barcode is but can be placed on another part of the product, cover the product with a blank label and put your label where it will fit on the product.

The products your about to send in should be secure. For things you don't want to get damaged in the warehouse like books and board games. Use stretch wrap or bubble wrap to keep them safe.

If the item is boxed well and will not get damaged in transit, simply put the label on it and it's ready to be shipped.

If you're concerned about the item being damaged, put it in a clear poly bag or zip lock bag and make sure to put a suffocation label on the outside of any poly bag that has an opening of more than 3".

Or you can stretch wrap or bubble wrap the item; you do not need a suffocation label for a stretched wrapped item.

Now that you have your items labeled and prepared, return to seller central. Click the "continue button".

Keep in mind you also have to option to have Amazon label your products. At this time it costs $0.20 a product, it's your call.

Next you'll come to a screen that shows shipment names and the address where your different products would be delivered to if you approve the shipments. To approve the shipment click on the button that says "approve shipment".

Separate your items into the corresponding boxes using the pack lists. I sometimes like to print the pack list out and check off the items I'm putting into each box just to make sure all the items will be sent to the correct warehouse.

Then click on the button that says "work on shipment". On this page, you'll be able to add the weight and the dimension of the box that you'll be using to send your shipment into Amazon.

Most of the time the dimensions of the box are already on the box itself, if not use measuring tape to measure the bottom, top, and side of the box.

As far as the weight goes, now you see how important it is to use a scale that shows the weight on the outside so you can read the results right away.

Next, you'll see how much it will cost to ship the box. You can approve the amount and it will be credited to your Amazon account.

You will not be charged for this right away. Once you send your shipment off and you start getting sales, your sales will most likely cover the costs of your shipment.

Then print the box labels, there are two per box. They'll print on one piece of paper, make sure to cut out the labels and tape them to the box using clear tape. Make sure the labels are readable and scannable so your shipment can be processed correctly. I usually place one label under the other.

Or if you're using the sticker labels, simply tear off the stickers and place them on the box.

Then all you have to do is take your box over to UPS or a UPS carrier and you're good to go! Or, you can call and have UPS pick it up from your home.

Wow! Now you have sent your first shipment to FBA. If you take your box over to UPS make sure to get a receipt.

Argena Olivis
October 8, 2014 ·

My first FBA shipment... Be going to UPS tomorrow. Super excited 😃

I'll never forget the first shipment I sent into Amazon. It was a long time coming because I had to piece a ton of information together in order to make sure I was doing everything right.

After hours of research and uncertainty, I finally got it sent out. Good times! That's why I decided to put this guide together because I know what it's like to struggle with getting your first shipment out to FBA.

You can log into your seller account the next day and track

your shipment. Amazon will email you when your items have arrived and are actively listed on Amazon!

Chapter 6: Goal Setting, Tracking, and Scaling Your Business + FAQ's

If you want a real business, you're going to have to keep track of your profit and loss in order to see if you're actually making money or losing money.

You'll find that your items will sell over time; some things will sell faster than others. If you want to create a steady income stream with FBA, you have to create a schedule.

Schedule when you're going to go sourcing, what your budget is, and when you're going to list and send the items to the warehouse.

Goal Setting

Set goals. How much do you want to make per month? Once you have that goal find out how much product you need to sell per month in order to reach that goal.

For example: If you want to make $2,000 a month. You have a product that will sell for $20 and your profit is $13. How many would you need to sell per month in order to make $2,000? You'd need to sell about 153 products that month to meet your goal. Do the numbers!

Once you get the hang of it, you'll see what sells fast and you'll get to learn what to keep investing in. Sometimes you'll get a product on sale and you'll never find it for that price again, you just have to make a game of it and keep at it.

I suggest you start off with retail arbitrage and sourcing at thrift stores then start moving on to more advancing sourcing like wholesale, bundle creation, online arbitrage, private label products, and multipacks.

Tracking

For tax reasons, make sure to keep all your receipts and invoices from the products you purchase to resell.

Also, make sure to have a sourcing budget. How much do you want to spend a month on buying inventory for your business? Figure it out, write it down, and take action.

Make tracking easier on yourself by using a spreadsheet like Microsoft Excel or something similar like Open Office Spreadsheet (a free alternative); there are many programs you can use to track your inventory and sales.

Scaling Your Business

Always keep good records and keep an eye on what sells fast, and what sells a little slower but was worth it in the end.

Start getting creative and create your own listings once you get the hang of it.

Start creating multipacks. Multipacks are multiples of the same items in one listing.

Create bundles. Bundles are a group of related products in one listing.

Study and keep learning about reselling. Look up YouTube videos, read books, and always be taking action on what you learn.

FAQ's

Inventory Maintenance

Sometimes there may be complications with the inventory you send to Amazon. Products can be warehouse damaged or damaged in transit. I'm going to tell you how to fix any of these problems that occur.

Believe it or not, you can lose money by not keeping up with your inventory. Once your first shipment is complete you need to log into SellerCentral and see if all the inventory has arrived safely and is actively listed.

Unfillable Inventory

So once your inventory is in the warehouse, log in to seller central and hover over the tab at the top that says "inventory" and when the drop down menu pops out go to "manage FBA inventory".

	Condition		Price	Inbound	Fulfillable	Unfulfillable
· Gel	New	$	9.99	0	1	0
	New	$	15.00	0	1	0
Rare Diamonds (2 Packs)	New	$	12.00	0	0	0
	Collectible - Like New	$	10.75	0	1	0
NaturalShape) Silicone Nipples -	New	$	13.99	0	1	0
	Used - Like New	$	29.99	0	1	0
undle	New	$	24.99	0	3	0
	New	$	12.00	0	1	0
	New	$	40.00	0	1	0
ack - Sleeping Beauty with Tiny	New	$	15.99	0	0	0

Click on the column that says "unfulfillable" at the top to see if any of your inventories is marked as unfulfillable.

If you have any unfulfillable inventory it'll come to the top of the column and you'll see a red number in the unfulfillable column that tells you how many items are unfulfillable for that particular listing.

To see the reason why it's unfulfillable, click on the red number and Amazon will show the reason or "disposition".

There are five reasons why the warehouse workers will mark your product as unfulfillable:

1) Customer Damaged- This means a customer purchased your item and opened it or something similar and sent the item back to Amazon.

2) Defective- This is when a customer purchased an item and returned it back to Amazon, and Amazon has found that the item is now defective or "not working".

3) Warehouse Damaged- This is when your item was damaged by either workers or machines in the warehouse when they were unpacking your items.

4) Distributor Damaged- This is when your product was damaged in transit to the warehouse.

5) Expired- If you're selling in grocery or related categories your items may expire and will no longer be fillable by Amazon.

If it was Amazon's fault (warehouse damaged, distributor damaged) that your item was damaged, you have the option to create a removal order and have it destroyed and get a refund from Amazon, or you can have it sent back to you for a small fee. At the moment, the fee is $0.50 per item.

If the item was damaged by the customer Amazon will not reimburse you for it. Either have it destroyed, or get it sent back to you and depending on the damage you can send it back to Amazon and list it as a used item.

So every time you get a new shipment in, check back to make sure that all your items are marked fillable. It's your job to maintain your account; Amazon will not email you about this.

Fixing Inventory & Listings

There's more information that you need to be aware of. Sometimes Amazon will list some of your items as "stranded". This means that there is not an offer for the product that you sent into Amazon.

To see if you have any current inventory that needs to be fixed, go to the inventory drop down menu at the top of seller central and click on "manage inventory".

To the left, you'll see items that say: "fix suppressed listing" "improve listing quality" and "fix stranded inventory".

> ► Show my inventory
>
> ► Fix suppressed listings
>
> ► Improve listing quality
>
> Fix Stranded Inventory

Fix Suppressed Listings

These are listings that are not visible to customers on Amazon. The cause for this is usually because the listing itself contains incorrect information. Or it may be because it's missing important information.

When you click on the arrow that says fix suppressed listing, you'll see the different information you can update such as the image, brand name, or description and bullets.

Make the changes to the listing and relist your item on Amazon.

Improve Listing Quality

This is similar to a suppressed listing. What you do here is add more information or update information about the product.

Fix Stranded Inventory

This is when an item is either removed from Amazon because it's hazmat or the listing is blocked by the original owner of the product.

You can either create a removal order or fix the problem and try to relist your item on Amazon.

Dealing with returns

When an item is returned Amazon will send you an email that says "refund initiated". When you log into your account, you'll be able to see the reason for the return.

As soon as the return is initiated, Amazon automatically updates your balance and subtracts the amount of money that the customer paid for the item.

The customer that initiates a refund is supposed to return the item to Amazon, but this is not always the case. If the customer does not return the item within 45 days you can be reimbursed by Amazon.

So be sure to keep track of when a return is initiated so you can go in and get reimbursed.

To view your returns, log into your seller central account and click on the button that says "orders" and in the drop-down menu click on "manage returns."

Customer Feedback

Be sure that you are describing your items clearly and really give attention to the condition notes if you're selling a used item.

I try to stick to only new or items that are "like new" to avoid getting bad feedback.

Bad feedback can drastically slow down your sales, especially as a new seller. Many customers won't leave feedback at all so it's up to you to keep bad feedback from coming in.

When selling used items, always be generous with your listing. This means you may want to list an item that you know is "like new" as a "used very good". Always overdeliver to avoid getting bad feedback. Customers will appreciate what they get if they weren't expecting the item to be in such great condition.

You won't be able to move bad feedback on your seller account by yourself; either Amazon or the customer would have to remove it.

Amazon will only remove bad feedback if the customer was describing the product and their complaint was more of a "product review".

If you do get bad feedback, email the customer directly. You also have the option to go in and refund them for their purchase if they haven't already initiated a refund.

Try your best to make the customer happy by resolving the problem, keep in mind that you will have access to the customer's address just in case you want to go above and beyond and send them a replacement item or gift card.

Don't ask the customer to remove the bad feedback right away, first resolve the problem and make sure they're satisfied. Make sure to keep note of the emails between you and the customer so if they do say in the email that they'd like to remove the bad feedback then you have proof that you can send to Amazon.

Make it as easy as possible to have the customer remove the feedback; send a message on exactly how to remove it step-by-step.

You also have the option to respond to the customer's feedback so everyone can see what your response is to such a low rating. If you decide to do this make sure to explain that you tried contacting the customer and that you've already given them a refund.

Pricing

Make sure you keep good documentation of how much you paid for an item, how much it costs to send it over to Amazon, and how much the Amazon fees will be when it sells.

You always want to make sure what you're selling is profitable. At best, you want to break even if something goes wrong and your item does not sell right away.

Use tools such as the FBA calculator to calculate profit before you even purchase items.

Keep in mind that customers that spend $35 or more get free shipping on their orders.

You can manually reprice items in your inventory at any time. There are also automatic repricing tools.

Avoiding Oversized Products

Avoid larger storage fees by sending in products that are not oversized. This means they are less than 8x8x8 inches on each side.

If you do decide to sell oversized products make sure you will surely turn a profit.

Avoiding Storage Fees

After you have items in Amazon's warehouse for over a year, you start to accumulate long term storage fees.

To avoid this review your inventory every 90 days or so to see what's not selling. Consider lowering the price.

Commingled Inventory Explained

When signing up for your Amazon account, Amazon will ask you if you want to have commingled inventory or non-commingled inventory.

Commingled inventory or stickerless commingled inventory is when you send products to the Amazon fulfillment center without having to label them and the product will be mixed in with other seller's products of the same item.

In order for your items to qualify, they must:

- be new

- have a scannable bar code

- must be in the Amazon catalog

- can't be in categories that require approval

I personally think you should avoid commingled inventory because it's risky. You're assuming everyone using this service will take time to package and check their items thoroughly.

If a customer receives someone's item other than yours then you risk getting bad feedback if the item wasn't as described.

Afraid To Scan Items In Store

I was nervous too when I first started scanning items in the store. But then when my husband told me that no one is going to be worried about me because there are now programs where if a customer scans an item they get sales on that item.

For example: Target Cartwheel. Overall, no one is really thinking about you, and furthermore they have no idea what you're doing anyway. They're just trying to get what they need and get out of the store.

The more you do it, the more comfortable you'll begin to feel. Memorize your requirements for purchasing an item for resell so you know right off the back if you're going to get the item or not.

If you're still too shy to scan, just act like you're on your phone and look up the product by its name.

Item Has No Sales Rank

If an item has no sales rank, this means it never sold before. When you're just starting out avoid these items because you're not sure if it's profitable or not.

Conclusion

Thank you again for reading *Fulfillment By Amazon For Beginners*!

I hope this book was able to help you to start your Amazon FBA business.

The next step is to take action and start re-selling!

Finally, if you enjoyed this book, then I'd like to ask you for a favor, would you be kind enough to leave a review for this book on Amazon? It'd be greatly appreciated!

By reviewing this book you give me feedback on what I can approve on or what I've done well so I can greater understand the needs of my customers.

Also, by leaving me a review, it'll help the book sell more copies and inspire others to start selling on Amazon which can ultimately change lives for the better.

Thank you, I appreciate you, and good luck with your Amazon business!

Preview Of 'Amazon FBA: Reselling Strategies For More Income On FBA' Chapter 1: Multipacks

With regular listings on Amazon you're able to go to a retail store, find a product that's already listed, and then send that single product into Amazon. You also have the option to send more than one of that item into Amazon and sell them as a single unit.

But multipacks allow to get some leverage and stand out from all the other competing sellers for that product.

A multipack is having 2 or more of the same item in a single listing. This means the customer would not need to order two or more of the same item, but they simply buy multiples of that item for one particular price.

This, in turn, saves the customer money and time. They won't have to worry about reordering the product so often on Amazon if they buy a multipack of the item.

It also saves you money in Amazon Fees. Amazon charges fees per product and technically a multipack listing will be only one product.

This method gives you leverage because you are thinking ahead, this will also get you more income per item. And if you can list the multipack for $25 or more they will qualify for super saver shipping. Customers love this because they can get their items shipped to them earlier and save.

You can do multipack listings in the health and beauty category and in the grocery category. If you're not yet approved for these categories make sure to scroll down to the end of this book and get your free category approval video.

So let's get right into the process. The first thing you do is log into your seller account and go to **inventory > add a product.**

Next click on the button that says "create a new product".

Then select the category of item that you want to sell the multipack in. Keep in mind that only certain categories allow you to create multipacks. The main ones are health and beauty and groceries.

So, select the category that best fits the item you will be selling.

Then you'll end up on the product listing screen.

If you are selling a multipack for a product that's already listed on Amazon you can simply copy and paste most of the information for that listing since it's basically the same item.

Everywhere you see a red asterisk (*) you need to fill out that field in order for your listing to be accepted.

Product name: Copy and paste the name from the original listing into this box. Make sure to add the words "pack of ____" at the end. Make sure to emphasize the number of items in your multipack.

For example: Jolly Rancher Candy Assorted Flavors (Pack Of 3)

Brand Name: This is where you add the brand of the item you're selling. For example: General Mills, Equate, and Colgate are brand names.

Package Quantity: Make sure you put the number of items that are included in your multipack. <u>Do not leave this blank</u> or Amazon will think it's a single item.

EAN or UPC: If you're selling an item that's already listed on Amazon, you can use the same UPC code from the original listing of the item begin sold.

But, if this is the first time this item will be listed on Amazon you'll need to buy UPC codes. You can get a ton of UPC codes for cheap on Ebay. Search eBay for "Amazon UPC codes".

The rest of the information on this page is not necessary to fill out, but if you want to you can. It never hurts to include extra details about the product.

Now, click the "next" button at the end of the page or click on the tab that says "Other".

Condition: Add the item condition, if you're selling in the health and beauty or in the grocery categories the item must be in new condition to send it FBA.

Your Price: Add the price you'll be selling the multipack for. It's up to you what you feel should be the best price, but if the customer is buying a multipack they'd like to save a few dollars by buying more at one time.

It's great if you can get the price $25 or more so they can qualify for the super saver shipping.

For example: If an item is selling for $10 by itself and you want to do a multipack of 3. You can price your item as high as $30. But you may want to knock off $2-$5 to make the listing more appealing. I would sell that multipack for between $25-$27.

Quantity: Add the number of items in your multipack.

Shipping Method: Choose the radio button that says "I want Amazon to ship and provide customer service for my items if they sell".

Okay, you're finished with this section. Now click on the tab that says "Images".

Images: If the item you're creating a multipack for is

already on Amazon, you're able to use the image from that original listing. You do not have to take your own images unless the product is not yet listed on Amazon.

So if it is already listed, simply go over to that listing and right click on the image you want to use and save it to your computer. Then upload it to the listing that you're in the process of creating.

If you have to take your own images, make it on a white background. You only need an image of the product you're selling-- not an image of the multiple items in your multipack.

For example: If you're selling 3 packs of markers. You don't need to take a picture of the three packs of markers, just one pack of markers.

So once you have your image, click on the button that says "add image" and find the image file on your computer and upload it. You're able to list up to 7 pictures. So if you want to show the item from multiple angles (front, back, sides, etc.) then you can do so. But you're only required to have one. But keep in mind the more you have the better for the customer. Images must be 1000x500 pixels.

Description: You can copy and paste what's in the description for the other listing if there's already one created. If not, you'll have to create your own.

Key Product Features: You get five lines where you get to talk about your product's features. Features are your products' most important qualities and this information will be displayed as bullet points in your listing. Make sure you tell the customer the exact the number of the product they'll be receiving in one of those bullet points.

Product Description: You have a 2,000 character

max to explain your product in a general manner (not particularly the item).

Tip: Go to Google and search for Amazon best sellers and take a look at the listings there so you can get some ideas of what a good product description and features are.

Keywords: None of these fields are necessarily required but you do want to make sure you fill out the search terms so people will find your item. Unless, the item is already listed. If it's already listed just copy and paste.

If you have to come up with your own search terms, make sure you're thinking into the mind of the buyer. If you were searching for your item what would you type into the Amazon search bar? Those are the words you want to be using. Use descriptive words that people will likely be searching for.

The search terms and keywords are extremely important because this is how customers will be able to find your listing when shopping.

More Details: Here, you just fill in as much information as possible. The more the better.

Product dimensions: This is something you can't simply copy and paste because you have to measure your entire multipack's dimensions. Amazon needs to know this information because they like to know what size box to use in advance when packaging items. What I usually do is measure the dimensions using a tape measurer. You're going to need the products' length, height, and width.

Weight: Weigh the product using an appropriate scale. You can round up, but do not round down. If you haven't yet gotten a scale here is a checklist of the items you'll need to run your FBA business: http://www.argenaolivis.com/wp-content/uploads/2014/10/fbachecklist.pdf

Number of Items: Put the number of items that is included in your multipack.

Unit Count: Put the number of items that is included in your multipack.

Unit Count Type: Put down the material your product comes in (example: bag, bottle, jar, box, etc.)

Okay, once you're done filling in as much information as you can make sure you click on the button that says "save and finish". Next you'll come to the screen and you'll see your products' ASIN number, image, sku, and title.

You won't be able to view the listing right away. The typical wait is about 15 minutes. Once you check out the new listing, you should see on your image that Amazon has put an image that says how many of the item there is.

For example: If you have a 5 pack. Amazon should have a logo and sticker on your picture that says "5 pack". This makes it official.

So now you're done. You've created your multipack. Now all

you need to do is send it off to Amazon.

Make sure when you send the multipack in that you have something that can hold these items together. Either a clear poly bag or stretch wrap will do. If you're using a poly bag make sure to include a suffocation label. Also, make sure you have a sticker on each multipack that says "sold as set, do not separate".

Check Out My Other Books

Below you'll find some of my other popular books that are popular on Amazon and Kindle as well. You can visit <u>my author page</u> on Amazon to see other work done by me.

Amazon FBA: Reselling Strategies For More Income On FBA

How To Make Money Online Fast: Step By Step Instructions On How To Work From Home Using Proven Internet Marketing Strategies

You can simply search for these titles on the Amazon website to find them.

[Bonus] Download Your Amazon FBA Bundle Creation Course + Video On How To Get Approved In Gated Categories

In the Amazon bundles mini-course you'll learn how to create bundles for Amazon FBA, which leads to a more stable business model and less competition.

Also, get our free video on how to get approved in categories. You'll need this to take your business to the next level.

To Get Access Visit:

http://www.argenaolivis.com/fbaeBook

www.ingramcontent.com/pod-product-compliance
Lightning Source LLC
Chambersburg PA
CBHW071002180526
45168CB00003B/1253